Native Americans

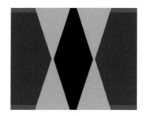

The Sioux

Richard M. Gaines

ABDO Publishing Company

visit us at
www.abdopub.com

Published by ABDO Publishing Company, 4940 Viking Drive, Suite 622, Edina, Minnesota 55435. Copyright © 2000 Abdo Consulting Group, Inc., Pentagon Tower, P.O. Box 36036, Minneapolis, Minnesota 55435 USA. International copyrights reserved in all countries. No part of this book may be reproduced in any form without written permission from the publisher.

Printed in the United States.

Illustrators: David Kanietakeron Fadden
Interior Photos: Corbis
Editors: Bob Italia, Tamara L. Britton, Kate A. Furlong
Art Direction & Maps: Pat Laurel
Border Design: Carey Molter/MacLean & Tuminelly (Mpls.)

Library of Congress Cataloging-in-Publication Data

Gaines, Richard M., 1942-
    The Sioux / Richard M. Gaines.
        p. cm. -- (Native Americans)
    Includes bibliographical references and index.
    Summary: Presents a brief introduction to the Sioux Indians including information on their homes, society, food, clothing, family life, and life today.
    ISBN 1-57765-382-3
    1. Dakota Indians--Juvenile literature. [1. Dakota Indians. 2. Indians of North America--Great Plains.] I. Title.

E99.D1 G35 2000
978.004'9752--dc21   00-023766

Contributing Editor: Barbara Gray, JD

Barbara Gray, JD (Kanatiyosh) is a member of the Mohawk Nation (Akwesasne), which is in New York State and Canada. Barbara earned her Juris Doctorate from Arizona State University College of Law in May of 1999. She is presently pursuing a Doctorate in Justice Studies that focuses on American Indian culture and issues at Arizona State University. When she finishes school, she will return home to the Mohawk Nation.

Illustrator: David Kanietakeron Fadden

David Kanietakeron Fadden is a member of the Akwesasne Mohawk Wolf Clan. His work has appeared in publications such as *Akwesasne Notes, Indian Time*, and the *Northeast Indian Quarterly*. Examples of his work have also appeared in various publications of the Six Nations Indian Museum in Onchiota, NY. His work has also appeared in "How The West Was Lost: Always The Enemy," produced by Gannett Production which appeared on the Discovery Channel. David's work has been exhibited in Albany, NY; the Lake Placid Center for the Arts; Centre Strathearn in Montreal, Quebec; North Country Community College in Saranac Lake, NY; Paul Smith's College in Paul Smiths, NY; and at the Unison Arts & Learning Center in New Paltz, NY.

Contents

Where They Lived

The Sioux are divided into three groups called the Dakota, Nakota, and Lakota. All three words mean "friend" or "ally."

The Ojibwa called the Dakota, Nakota, and Lakota people *Nadouessioux* (nay doo we sue). It means "little snakes" or "lesser enemies." In the 1700s, French traders and trappers shortened this Ojibwa word to "Sioux."

The Black Hills of South Dakota

Many Sioux creation stories say the Sioux homelands were in the Black Hills of present-day South Dakota. Others say the people came from the woodlands of present-day northern Minnesota. By the time the Europeans arrived in America, the Dakota, Nakota, and Lakota controlled most of the **Great Plains**.

Many Dakota lived in the woodlands. But, some lived on the prairies. The Nakota lived on the prairies southwest of the Dakota. The Lakota lived west of the Nakota in the Black Hills. The Lakota lands had prairies and forested mountains. The Lakota people are known as the caretakers of the sacred Black Hills.

The Sioux Homelands

Detail Area

WOODLANDS

MINNESOTA

BLACK HILLS

SOUTH DAKOTA

Society

The Sioux are divided into seven **bands**, which speak Dakota, Nakota, or Lakota. These seven bands make up the Seven **Council** Fires (*Oceti Sakowin*). They united the Dakota, Nakota, and Lakota speakers as one large society. The Seven Council Fires gathered to socialize and discuss important issues.

Each band in the Seven Council Fires was divided into seven smaller bands. They had their own council fires. And, each of these bands was organized into a *tiyospaye*, or "a group of dwellings."

Each *tiyospaye* was a small group of extended families. It included mothers, fathers, children, aunts, uncles, cousins, and grandparents. It also included others who chose to live with the group and those the group had adopted.

Sioux leaders were called *itacan*. They were respected men of the band. They were chosen because of their strength, wisdom, and love of their people. These leaders did not have the power to tell others what to do. Decisions were made during **council** fire meetings.

The holy man, or *wicasa wakan*, was also respected. He had great power and healed the people with herbs and ceremonies. The people also went to the *wicasa wakan* for spiritual advice.

The *akicita* was made up of young men. They organized hunts and kept order. The *akicita* were like modern-day police.

A Sioux tiyospaye

Homes

The Nakota and Lakota lived in tipis. Some Dakota lived in tipis, too. But, many others lived in wigwams. Wigwams had an arched wooden frame covered with bark, thatch, or animal skins.

Tipis are cone-shaped homes. They have a pointed top and the bottom forms a circular floor. A woman could put up or take down a tipi in less than a day.

Tipi frames were made of pine poles. Three long poles were raised to form the tipi's frame. Eight to ten more poles were added to fill out the frame.

Once the frame was finished, it was covered with buffalo hides. An average sized tipi used about 15 buffalo hides. These hides had been prepared and sewn into one piece. The covering was stretched across the frame. It was held together with wooden pins. The bottom of the covering was held down with stakes or rocks.

The top of the tipi had two flaps that allowed smoke to escape from the fire pit. All tipi doors faced east to greet the morning sun and honor the first direction.

Several tipis were set up in a circle. The center of the circle was called a *hocoka*. The *hocoka* was an important place. It was where all four directions came together.

The Sioux used tipi poles to make **travois**. Travois could carry heavy loads. The Sioux used dogs to pull the travois. Each dog could carry 30 to 50 pounds (14 to 23 kg). In the 1600s, horses were available to the Sioux. The Sioux used them to haul the travois. A horse travois could carry the **elderly** and the sick.

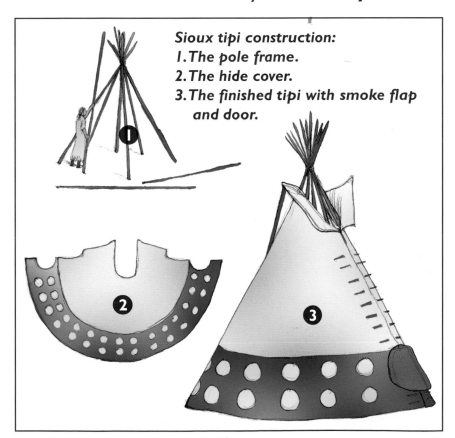

Sioux tipi construction:
1. *The pole frame.*
2. *The hide cover.*
3. *The finished tipi with smoke flap and door.*

9

Food

The Sioux ate what they could find in their homelands. The eastern Dakota had a diet that included wild rice, duck, deer, elk, berries, and other woodland plants, birds, and animals.

In the Great Plains, people ate fruits, berries, roots, and vegetables they found growing wild. They also hunted antelope, deer, grouse, turkey, and other prairie animals.

Buffalo was also an important food. They were mostly hunted in the fall. No part of the buffalo was wasted. It was eaten and made into clothing, tipi coverings, shields, and weapons.

Some meats were eaten right away. Others were **preserved**. To preserve the meat, the Sioux hung it in strips on drying poles. This dried meat, or jerky, was stored. It could be eaten throughout the winter.

The Sioux also made pemmican from dried meat, dried berries, dried fruits, nuts, and melted buffalo fat. The meat, berries, fruit, and nuts were crushed. Melted buffalo fat was poured over this mixture.

Pemmican was stored in animal bladders and intestines. These containers were lightweight, watertight, and safe from insects. It made pemmican easy to take on trips.

The Sioux hunted buffalo for food.

Clothing

A Sioux shirt

The Sioux made clothes from different animals found in their homelands.

Sioux men wore **breechcloths** and thigh-length leggings. The leggings often had **fringes** or porcupine quills along the outside seam. Sometimes, leggings were painted red.

Men wore shirts made from one whole animal hide. The hide was sewn under the arms to make loose sleeves. The sleeves and the bottom of the shirt had long fringes. The shirts were decorated with porcupine quills, beads, hair locks, or animal tails.

Men wore hats made from animal skins. They often attached horns to the hat. The men also wore hats with feathers. Eagle feathers were earned for deeds. It took a person a long time to earn enough feathers for an eagle feather war bonnet.

Women wore deerskin dresses and skirts. The dresses were sewn from two or three animal skins. The **hem** and sleeves had fringes. Some dress tops had quill work, beads, elk teeth, or seashell decorations.

Sioux men and women wore moccasins. Sometimes, they made them from buffalo hides that still had the fur attached. In the winter, these moccasins could be turned with the fur inside, which kept their feet warm. Men and women also wore buffalo-hide robes and animal-skin **sashes**.

A Sioux family in traditional clothing

Crafts

A beaded vest

Sioux women were skilled at making clothes. They often decorated them with porcupine quills.

Quills are hard and needed to be softened so the women could make them into a geometric design. To soften the quill, a woman placed it in her mouth and pulled it through her teeth. This flattened the quill. She had to work fast as she sewed the quill into her design. As the quill dried, it became hard again. Quilling took a lot of skill, time, and patience.

In the 1600s, women began to decorate clothing with European glass beads. Quilling was still done, but beading was quicker and easier.

Sioux women did a beading stitch that is called the "lazy stitch." The bead work was laid down in rows and sewn into place. The needle never passed all the way through the leather.

This was done so the stitches could not be seen from the other side.

The women also decorated bags, pouches, **sashes**, and **cradleboard** covers with beautiful bead and quill work. Today, the Sioux still create beautiful bead and quill work.

A Sioux cradleboard

Sioux men painted tipi covers. When a tipi was ready to be painted, the owner announced a feast. He invited friends and other tribesmen who specialized in the art of tipi painting. The men sang songs and invited spirits to help them decorate the new tipi.

The tipi cover was laid out on the ground. Then, the men drew designs on the hide. They used pens made from buffalo bones. They made paint from clay and rocks.

Sioux women doing quill work.

Family

Kinship is important to the Sioux. They believe that they are related not only to their human family, but also to the sun, wind, birds, plants, animals, trees, and the rest of nature.

The Sioux also believe that protecting their extended family and nature is their job. To do this, they perform ceremonies and **rituals**. They also use ceremonies and rituals to retain balance and restore harmony with nature.

Sioux families followed many rules. These rules made life more comfortable for everyone. An open tipi door meant anyone was welcome to visit. A closed door meant the family wanted to be alone.

Inside the tipi, men sat cross-legged along the north wall. Women sat on their knees along the south side. Guests sat outside the tipi until asked in. Then, guests sat to the left of the head of the family.

During meals, men were served first. The Sioux did not use forks. They ate with their fingers. Dinner guests had to bring their own plates and cups. They were expected to eat everything served to them.

Life inside a tipi

Children

A Sioux doll

Sioux children ran and played wherever they wanted. Their families taught them how to be generous, respectful, and patient.

Mothers and grandmothers taught girls how to make clothes and complete other important tasks. They also made tiny **cradleboards** for their dolls. Dolls taught girls how to care for babies.

Boys learned skills that helped them to become good warriors and hunters. An uncle or grandmother often gave a boy his first bow and arrows.

Sioux children liked to play hoop games. One game used a webbed hoop and a forked stick. The hoop was made from ash wood and leather. Sinew was woven around the hoop to create a web. At the web's center was a hole called the heart.

Children threw the hoop in the air or rolled it along the ground. Then, they tried to throw a stick through the hoop's heart. Usually teams played against each other. This game taught boys the skills needed to be good hunters.

Boys also played a game called "Throwing-Them-Off-Their-Horses." Boys from one **band** would gallop toward a group from another band. When the groups met, the boys tried to throw each other from the horses. Anyone thrown to the ground was considered dead. The game ended when all the riders from one side were on the ground.

Children playing a hoop game

Myths

The following is the story of the Sacred White Buffalo Calf Woman. The story tells of her message, her gift of the sacred pipe, and her promise to return to the Sioux.

Long ago in a time of great hunger, two warriors left the camp to hunt. Soon, they saw a beautiful woman with hair that hung down to the ground. The woman sent them back to their camp to tell the people that she was coming with great gifts.

The next day, the woman appeared in the camp. She stayed for four days, and taught them many ceremonies. She told them they could eat the buffalo. But, she told them not to eat snakes, lizards, toads, eagles, crows, or hawks.

She gave them the Buffalo Calf Pipe to smoke during ceremonies and **council** meetings. The pipe's smoke would carry a person's prayers to *Wakan Tanka*, the Great Spirit.

Before leaving, the woman promised to return to the people once during each age and bring them peace. As the people watched, the beautiful woman changed into a black buffalo. Next, she changed into a red-brown buffalo. Then, she changed into a yellow buffalo. Finally, the woman changed into a white buffalo and disappeared.

Today, the Sioux await the return of the Sacred White Buffalo Calf Woman.

The Sacred White Buffalo Calf Woman holds the Buffalo Calf Pipe.

War

The Sioux were excellent warriors. They fought bravely to protect their people. In war, they carried a shield and a lance, or a bow and arrows.

Shields were made from thick buffalo hide. Each warrior painted his shield with designs that came to him during a vision or dream. Women were not allowed to touch any Sioux weapons.

Men wore breast plates made from small bones. These bones acted like armor and kept arrows or lances from piercing the chest. Sometimes, the breast plates were made from buffalo horn hair pipes. Warriors also wore hair pipe chokers to protect their necks while in battle.

The Sioux were excellent riders. Their horses were well trained and fast. Their horses allowed the men to move quickly in battle and out of danger. Later, the Sioux traded with Europeans to get guns. Then, they became excellent **marksmen**.

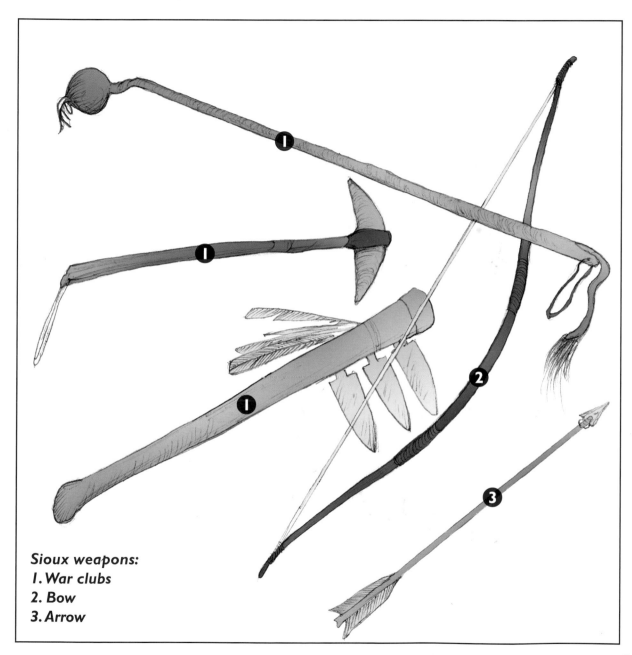

Sioux weapons:
1. War clubs
2. Bow
3. Arrow

Contact with Europeans

In 1540, Spaniard Francisco Vásquez de Coronado's **expedition** for gold took him into Colorado. It is very likely that he met the Lakota during those travels.

Spaniards introduced the Sioux to horses. Many of the Spaniard's horses escaped. It was not long before the Sioux had horses. They called the horses *sunka wakan,* which means "sacred dogs."

The Sioux housing and food changed after they got horses. They began to live in tipis and to hunt buffalo. The horse made these things possible.

In 1654, French explorer Pierre Espirit Radisson met the Dakota in present-day Minnesota. Radisson found five large Dakota villages with about 5,000 people.

On August 27, 1804, the Lewis and Clark Expedition met the Nakota. Lewis wrapped an American flag around a Nakota baby born that day. He proclaimed the child an American. That child, Strike the Ree, remained a friend to the United States all his life.

The French and Americans brought cloth, brass kettles, flour, coffee, glass beads, and guns to trade with the Sioux. The Sioux traded furs, quill and bead work, and other goods.

The Sioux encounter a Spanish explorer.

Sitting Bull

Sitting Bull was born in present-day South Dakota in 1831. At age 14, he went on his first war party. Because of his bravery, he received the name Sitting Bull. Soon, he became a respected **medicine man**. Then, in 1867, he became a Hankapa Lakota chief.

Sitting Bull led his people to many victories in the Great Sioux War of 1876. That year, the U.S. wanted to buy Sioux land. They thought the land had gold in it. But, the Sioux did not want to sell their **sacred** land.

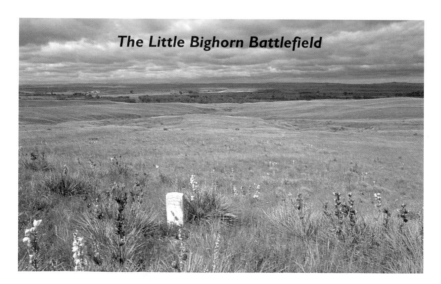

The Little Bighorn Battlefield

The U.S. government sent Lieutenant Colonel George Armstrong Custer and his troops to fight the Sioux. There were many bloody battles.

The most famous battle was called the Battle of the Little Bighorn. It was fought on June 25, 1876. In this battle, Sitting Bull and another warrior named Crazy Horse surrounded Custer's troops. In less than an hour, Custer and all of his troops had been killed.

Sitting Bull

After this battle, Sitting Bull feared for his people's lives. So, he led them to safety in Canada. But, the Sioux almost starved there. So, Sitting Bull and the Sioux returned to the U.S. in 1881. They lived at the Standing Rock **Reservation**.

In 1889, Sitting Bull learned of the Ghost Dance. He believed the dance would unite the Sioux. He also believed it would return the life they had before the Europeans arrived in America. Sitting Bull encouraged his people to perform the dance.

The U.S. government **banned** the Ghost Dance. They feared it would bring more wars. In 1890, police arrested Sitting Bull. His warriors tried to rescue him. But, Sitting Bull was killed. He is buried in Mobridge, South Dakota.

The Sioux Today

In 1868, the U.S. government and the Sioux signed a **treaty**. It gave the *Paha Sapa,* or the Black Hills, to the Sioux. But in 1877, the Sioux were driven from the Black Hills. U.S. citizens then settled there.

In 1974, the Indian Claims Court said the Sioux had not been properly paid for the loss of the Black Hills. In 1980, the U.S. Supreme Court agreed and awarded the Sioux $106 million for the land.

Oglala Sioux Nation President Harold Salway meets with U.S. President Bill Clinton at the Pine Ridge Reservation in South Dakota.

The Sioux refused the money. They said, "The Black Hills are not for sale." Today, they continue to fight for the return of the Black Hills.

The Sioux live on **reservations** in South Dakota, North Dakota, Nebraska, and Minnesota. These reservations have about 106,500 members.

For most Sioux, reservation life is hard. Some homes have poor plumbing. Some do not have telephones. Many people are poor and out of work.

Some Sioux have cattle ranches and farms. They also run **cultural** centers and recreation departments. Recreation departments give guided tours for hunting and fishing.

The Sioux have **pow-wows** every summer. These meetings include **rodeos**, concerts, dances, and sporting activities.

Mike Caughey performs the Lakota Men's Traditional dance at an Earth Day festival celebration.

The Pretty Lodge Singers from the Spirit Lake Sioux Reservation.

29

In 1994, Miracle, the white buffalo, was born. To the Sioux, this is a sign that peace and harmony will soon return.

The Sioux are a strong, spiritual people. They still have great pride in their history and **culture**. They are working hard to **preserve** their **traditional** ways of life, their language, and their rights.

Jay Taken Alive of the Standing Rock Sioux tribe says a prayer after the return of an 80-year-old golden eagle headdress.

Miracle, a white female buffalo calf, stands with its mother.

Howard Studhorse chops wood at a Sioux camp along the Missouri River in South Dakota.

Glossary

ban - to forbid.
band - a number of persons acting together; a subgroup of a tribe.
breechcloth - a simple garment worn by men to cover their loins; a loincloth.
council - a group of people who meet, usually to make decisions.
cradleboard - a decorated flat board with a wooden band at the top that protects the
    baby's head.
culture - the customs, arts, and tools of a nation or people at a certain time.
elder - a person having authority because of age or experience.
expedition - a journey for a special purpose, such as exploration or scientific study.
fringe - a border or trim made of threads or cords, either loose or tied together in small
    bunches.
Great Plains - a region east of the Rocky Mountains in the United States and Canada.
hem - a border or edge of a garment.
marksman - a person who shoots well.
medicine man - a spiritual leader of a tribe or nation.
pow-wow - a council or conference of Native Americans.
preserve - to keep from harm or change.
reservation - a tract of land that is set aside by the government for Native
    American tribes.
ritual - a form or system of rites.
rodeo - a contest or exhibition of skill in roping cattle or riding horses and bulls.
sacred - holy.
sash - a long, broad strip of cloth or ribbon, worn as an ornament around the waist or
    over one shoulder.
tradition - the handing down of beliefs, customs, and stories from parents to children.
travois - a frame of two wooden poles tied together over the back of an animal and
    allowed to drag on the ground. It was used to transport loads.
treaty - a formal agreement between nations.

Web Sites

Lakota na Dakota Wowapi Oti Kin (Lakota Dakota Information Home Page):
   http://puffin.creighton.edu/lakota/index.html
Standing Rock Sioux Tribe: **http://www.standingrock.org/**

These sites are subject to change. Go to your favorite search engine and type in "Sioux" for more sites.

Index